4.1
.5

P9-DWU-917

JAMIE
BESTWICK

EXTREME SPORTS STARS

BY MATT SCHEFF

abdopublishing.com
An Imprint of Abdo Publishing
abdopublishing.com

www.abdopublishing.com

Published by Abdo Publishing, a division of ABDO, PO Box 398166,
Minneapolis, Minnesota 55439. Copyright © 2015 by Abdo
Consulting Group, Inc. International copyrights reserved in
all countries. No part of this book may be reproduced in
any form without written permission from the publisher.
SportsZone™ is a trademark and logo of Abdo Publishing.

Printed in the United States of America,
North Mankato, Minnesota
042014
092014

Cover Photos: Cody York Photography
(foreground, background)
Interior Photos: Cody York Photography,
1, 6, 7, 8-9, 10, 11, 12-13, 14-15, 16-17,
18-19, 20-21, 22-23, 24-25, 26-27, 28, 29,
30 (left), 31; AP Images, 4-5, 30 (right)

Editor: Chrös McDougall
Series Designer: Maggie Villaume

Library of Congress Control Number: 2014933912

Cataloging-in-Publication Data
Scheff, Matt.
 Jamie Bestwick / Matt Scheff.
   p. cm. -- (Extreme sports stars)
Includes index.
ISBN 978-1-62403-456-5
1. Bestwick, Jamie, 1971- --Juvenile literature. 2.
Cyclists--United States--Biography--Juvenile literature.
3. Bicycle motocross--United States--Biography--Juvenile
literature. I. Title.
796.04/092--dc23
[B]
                    2014933912

CONTENTS

WINNING WITH FLAIR

The crowd was on its feet for the BMX Vert Best Trick event at the 2005 X Games. The top riders in BMX were showing off their most daring tricks. But no one could match Jamie Bestwick. The rising star dropped in and started building up huge air.

Jamie competes in the Freestyle Vert finals at the 2005 X Games.

Jamie waves to the crowd after a performance at the X Games.

Jamie does a downside tailwhip at the 2007 X Games.

Jamie launched into the air one last time. While holding the handlebars, he whipped his bike around in two full spins while he did a backflip. In a flash, Jamie was back on his seat, just as the tires landed on the halfpipe. It was a double tailwhip flair! No BMX rider had ever landed that trick in competition before. Jamie was soon named the gold-medal winner.

Jamie performs on the vert ramp at an X Games event in Brazil.

FAST FACT

Jamie won his first BMX competition in 1987.

EARLY LIFE

Jamie Bestwick was born on July 8, 1971, in Nottingham, United Kingdom. As a kid, Jamie loved to ride bikes. By age 10, he was already doing simple BMX tricks such as jumping off of curbs. But riding was just a hobby.

Jamie graduated from high school. Then he took a job as a mechanic for an airline company. He got married, too. Jamie was happy with his life. But he never stopped riding BMX. He still competed for fun.

Jamie talks to the crowd after a performance at the 2010 X Games.

Jamie turns upside down during his run at the 2010 X Games.

Jamie flies into the air no-handed while performing on a vert ramp.

RISING STAR

Jamie was one of the rising stars in BMX. He won the World Championships in 1991. In 1996, he entered the X Games for the first time. He won a bronze medal when he finished third in the Freestyle Vert event.

Jamie shows off
a move.

In 1999, Jamie became a full-time BMX rider. He quit his job, packed his things, and moved to the United States. There, he could train with and compete against the top riders in the world, including BMX legend Dave Mirra.

FAST FACT

Jamie took a sponsorship deal with GT Bikes. The company paid him to use and endorse its equipment.

Jamie performs a turndown flair at the 2007 X Games.

In 2000, Jamie won his first X Games gold medal. He thrilled the crowd in his first run with a series of huge airs. Then, in his final run, he landed the first turndown flair ever in competition. To do the trick, Jamie did a complete flip and spin while in the air.

Jamie kept blazing new ground in freestyle. In 2003, he nailed the first tailwhip flair at the X Games Global Championships. Two years later, he stunned the X Games crowd with his famous double tailwhip flair. BMX fans were always wondering what he'd do next.

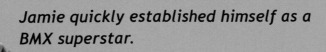

Jamie quickly established himself as a BMX superstar.

Jamie shows off his Freestyle Vert gold medal at the 2008 X Games.

BEST OF THE BEST

Jamie was almost unbeatable. In 2005, he won every competition he entered. That included gold medals at the X Games and the Dew Tour championship. And he just kept going. At times, it seemed like no one could stop him.

FAST FACT

In 2005, Jamie missed an event on the Dew Tour because of the birth of his son, Samuel. But he was perfect in the other events and won the tour anyway!

In 2006, Jamie thought about retiring from BMX. He wasn't enjoying it. But he kept at it and rediscovered how much fun it was.

Jamie gets big air on the vert ramp while practicing at the 2009 X Games.

By 2007, Jamie was already in his mid 30s. BMX freestyle is usually a sport dominated by younger athletes. But Jamie's best was yet to come. In 2007, he won gold at the X Games for Freestyle Vert. And he won the event again each of the next six years!

Jamie has been dominant on the Dew Tour. In 2013, the 41-year-old busted out his famous big air to score an amazing 94.00 at the Dew Tour final vert event. The huge run gave him his ninth straight championship!

Jamie poses for the cameras at a 2013 X Games stop in Brazil.

Jamie throws down a Superman Indian Air at the 2010 X Games.

GREATEST OF ALL TIME

Who is the greatest BMX rider of all time? Mat Hoffman helped make the sport what it is today. Dave Mirra brought it to a new level. But for pure dominance, no one can touch Jamie Bestwick. Since he turned pro in the late 1990s, nobody has been able to match him.

Jamie has won nine Dew Tour BMX vert titles through 2013. He has 13 X Games Medals—11 of them gold. Even into his early 40s, he dominates a sport in a way few athletes ever have. He has taken BMX freestyle to levels many would have thought impossible 20 years ago. No one knows when he will finally retire. But it's certain that when he does, his skills on a BMX bike won't soon be forgotten.

The tuck no-hander is one of Jamie's setup tricks.

Jamie flies into the air and kicks the bike all the way around, pulling a trick known as a tailwhip.

TIMELINE

1971

Jamie Bestwick is born on July 8 in Nottingham, United Kingdom.

1987

Jamie wins his first BMX competition.

1991

Jamie wins the World Championships.

1996

Jamie enters his first X Games and wins a bronze medal in Vert Freestyle.

1999

Jamie quits his job and begins to ride BMX full time.

2000

Jamie wins his first X Games gold medal.

2005

Jamie wins gold at the X Games and his first Dew Tour title.

2013

Jamie wins his ninth straight Dew Tour title and his eighth straight X Games gold medal.

GLOSSARY

Best Trick
An event in which the rider is scored based on the best trick he or she lands.

BMX
Short for bicycle motocross; it is a style of bicycle originally designed for dirt racing.

BMX freestyle
A form of competition in which athletes do tricks on their BMX bikes.

double tailwhip flair
A BMX freestyle trick in which a rider spins the bike around twice while doing a backflip.

endorse
When a famous person promotes a company or a product in exchange for money or other benefits.

flair
When both a rider and the bike do a backflip and a 180-degree spin.

halfpipe
A type of ramp used in BMX freestyle, shaped like the letter U.

retire
To stop doing something for a living.

vert
Short for vertical; in BMX freestyle, vert is a type of event held on a halfpipe with tall, vertical walls.

INDEX